Quilting Designs from Antique Quilts

by Pepper Cory

Acknowledgements

Many thanks to Bonnie Bus, Rebecca Haarer, Pat McGinn, my mother Mary Peddie, Rod Magyar and Anita Phillips for their advice and support. And special recognition and gratitude to the following people and institutions who so kindly gave me permission to use their designs: Carrow and McNerney Antiques, Jan and Larry Fisher, Mrs. Ora (Ruby) Hostetler, the Michigan Historical Museum, David Pottinger, Bruce and Charlotte Riddle, Linda Ruether, Julie Silber, Misses Lydia and Minnie Yoder.

Quilting Designs from Antique Quilts
Copyright © 1987 by Pepper Cory
Published by C & T Publishing
P.O. Box 1456
Lafayette, CA 94549

All rights reserved. No part of this work covered by the copyright hereon may be reproduced or used in any form or by any means—graphics, electronic, or mechanical, including photocopying, recording, taping, or information storage and retrieval systems—without written permission of the publisher.

ISBN 0-914881-08-6
Library of Congress Card Catalog Number 87-071887

Printed in the United States of America

Credits

Cover artwork and calligraphy by Kathryn Darnell, Darnell Calligraphy & Illustration.

Graphic layout by Diana Grinwis, Grinwis Art Service, East Lansing, Michigan.

Typesetting by Mary Christine/Capital Typography, Lansing, Michigan.

Table of Contents

Dedication	3
Forward	4
How to be a better quilt marker	5
Univerjat	7
Lancaster County Stencils	14
Miller Auction Boxes	18
Carrow and McNerney	30
Michigan Historical Museum Quilt	31
Shipshe Auction Quilt	36
Riddle Quilt	37
Playing with Patterns	38
Fisher Quilt	40
Silber/Ruether Quilts	42
Ruby Hostetler	48
Yoder Sisters	52
Pottinger Collection	53
How to find the right size pattern	64
References and resources	64
About the author	64

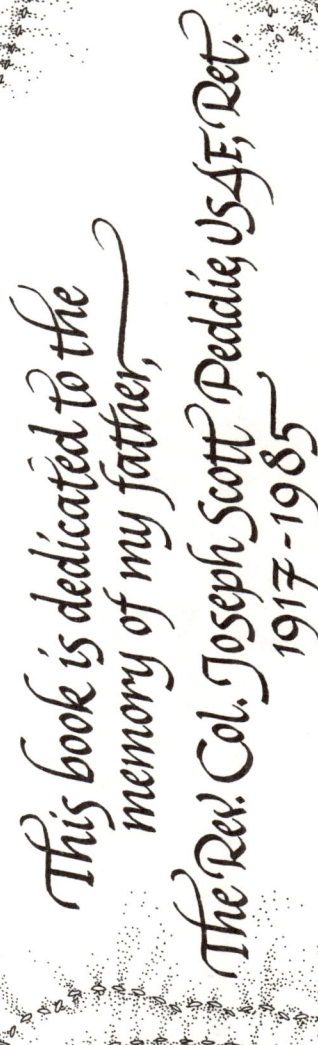

This book is dedicated to the memory of my father,
The Rev. Col. Joseph Scott "Peddie" USAF, Ret.
1917-1985

Forward

This book is for quilt lovers. They come in all shapes, sizes and ages—historians who appreciate quilts as artifacts from the past, collectors who search out rare antique quilts, designers who adore the graphics of quilts-as-art, quiltmakers still making their own quilts and carrying on the tradition of fine workmanship, the admirers who hang quilts on walls and the children who like to snuggle under them, and, lastly, this book is for the dreamers who, one day, want to make a quilt.

Handquilting gives a quilt a soft dimension—dimension being that quality which elevates the quilt from a flat fabric canvas to a concentration wavor? Isn't it a pain to produce work of art that has depth, warmth, and tactile attraction. You know how hard it is to keep your hands off quilts at a quilt show! Handquilting seems to lay over the surface of a quilt a soft spider web of stitches. It gently elevates some parts of the fabric to your sight while lowering other parts into shadows. You might get the idea I deplore machine quilting. Not so—there is definitely a place for handquilting work. However, I'm making a case for handquilting so that people who may not have tried it, or who have dismissed the craft, will look again at its positive points. To make a comparison, machine quilting makes a very definite line on the fabric, rather like the blacker, thicker stroke of an ink pen, while handquilting resembles a grey pencil line. And there are several drawbacks to machine quilting. If you have an average sewing machine, you must choose a flat batting so that your piece will feed smoothly through the machine, and for most sewers, complex or curved designs are difficult to machine stitch. And lastly, machine quilting limits you to the location of the machine. If you baste the layers of your quilt well—the top, batting, and backing—you can haul it around with you. You can handquilt anywhere—curled on the couch, propped up in bed, at your friend's house, even riding on an airplane! How's that for "quality" time? Which brings me back to the Time controversy...

As the search for patterns progressed, I asked myself, "What is the attraction of handquilting?" Quilting is, after all, a job that a sewing machine can, technically, do in a much shorter time. Like the devil's advocate might point out, what about all the **time** involved in handquilting? We are told constantly that time is money, you need to work hard and play hard, you must spend quality time with your children, etc. But, before I tackle the big Time question, let me share with you what I think handquilting adds to a quilt from an artist's standpoint.

When I started to seek out designs for this book, I quickly came to realize I needed to look at quilts with "X-ray eyes." It is easy to love an attractive colorful quilt—less easy to appreciate the subtlety of the handquilting on a worn-out, raggedy quilt. To look just at the stitching, I had to erase from my mind the color and piecing of the quilts I handled. And on several occasions, it was literally the handling, the feel, of the quilt—the weight of the thousands of stitches—that alerted me to the designs hidden in the fabric. The "skeleton" of the quilt was its handquilting and that was what I sought.

Again, the questions arise—don't you get impatient as you handquilt? Doesn't your concentration wavor? Isn't it a pain to produce small, even stitches? In short, isn't it a **bore** to handquilt? For me, the answer is an emphatic NO! As I handquilt, the work becomes a soothing meditative activity. By its very repetitive nature, quilting is relaxing. I do some of my best thinking as I quilt, sometimes even problem-solving. Somewhere I heard that Einstein jotted down his famous equation, $E=MC^2$, as he was eating breakfast, and that one of the discoverers of DNA came up with his breakthrough insight as he was riding on the bus. Although I don't lay claim to any earth-shaking ideas as the result of my handquilting, I do recognize that my mind is calmer after a spell of quilting. It also subdues my minor vices—I can't drink a cup of coffee, smoke a cigarette, eat a pastry, or bite my nails as I handquilt! And the big bonus is that, needle-full by needle-full, the stitches appear, bringing me surely closer to the completion of my latest masterpiece.

Julie Silber, the curator of the Esprit quilt collection, offered this thoughtful insight as to why people, in this modern age, still handquilt. She said, "I bet that if you hooked up a quilter to a bio-feedback machine, it would show that she produces Alpha waves as she quilts." I knew it felt good! When I quit my job as a substance abuse therapist, a colleague wrote me the nicest note. He said "You won't be keeping alcoholics out of the bars or addicts off the streets, but who knows how many people you might 'turn on' to quilting?"

The designs in this book were drawn from antique quilts and patterns all over the U.S.—Indiana, Michigan, Ohio, Illinois, Pennsylvania, New York, and points unknown. Many of the designs are beautiful—curve-y elaborate fantasies of flowers and vines—while others are whimsical, like the rooster on the cover of this book. Each of them has expanded my knowledge and appreciation of handquilting. I hope you like these designs and that you use them. They are not simply records of antique work—they are inspirations for us here and now. I hope they make you so excited that you want to immediately sit down and stitch. That's the whole idea.

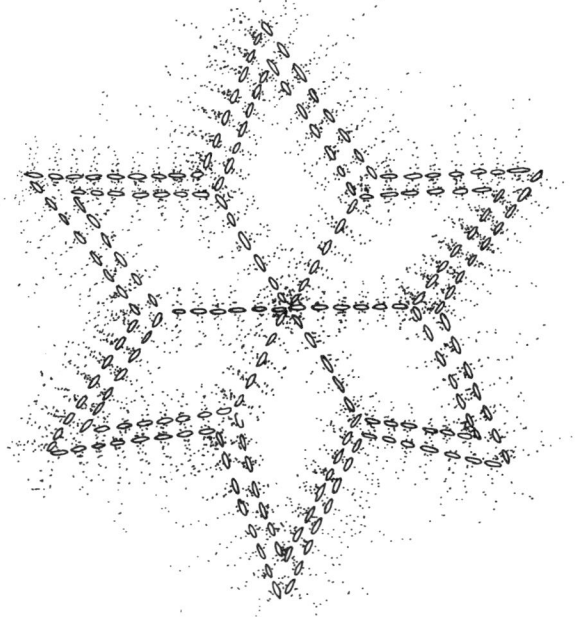

How to be a Better Quilt Marker

I hope that you are reading this section after you have perused the patterns in this book and gotten all excited about the new (old) designs, but **before** you mark your quilt top. Because it's time to look at your quilt top, really look, and visualize what quilting can do for your creation.

Before choosing any quilting patterns, spread your top out—on the floor, over the biggest bed in the house, or best of all, pin or tape the top to a wall. Now get back and look at it. Pull up a chair and spend some time looking at it. And then be honest with yourself. There will be some areas of the quilt which do not merit "fancy" designs. Plain, or filler, quilting will be the best choice for most pieced blocks. Consider this—why should you spend time quilting a complex design on a part of your quilt where it won't show?

There are three quilting choices for pieced blocks. The first is quilting "by the piece." This means quilting a quarter inch in (or less if the pieces are tiny) from the shapes in the pieced blocks. This avoids the problem of quilting over the seams in the block. First cousin to the "quarter inch in" method is "in the ditch" quilting. This is quilting as close as possible to the seams of the block. When "in the ditch" quilting is done well, the quilter avoids the seam allowance problem by skipping to the other side of the seam as she feels the extra thickness of cloth underneath. This means your quilting line moves over slightly—perhaps 1/16 of an inch. This difference is not enough to be noticed by anyone but you. Relax.

Another method of quilting pieced blocks, and the way the majority of antique pieced quilts were quilted, is to mark plain quilting—or filler quilting—over the blocks, disregarding the seams in the blocks. The most common plain quilting was parallel lines, running across the block, 1/2 to 1 inch apart. A clear plastic ruler (there are several good ones on the market) is your best tool. When you mark lines in a cross across the block making little squares, it is called crosshatching. (Illustration 1) When you mark in X lines that do not meet at right angles but produce diamond shapes, it is called a "hanging diamond" pattern. (See Illustration 2) I believe many antique pieced quilts were marked like this for several good reasons. Close plain quilting gave strength to the quilt. Remember sometimes old fabrics (read fragile) were re-cycled in these quilts and also that old-fashioned battings did not have the bonding our modern quilt bats do. Close plain quilting required less stopping and starting than "by the piece" quilting. Our ancestors were as aware as we are today of the time required to quilt their tops. Plain quilting was just plain faster. Another reason is that most antique quilts were quilted on a quilting frame at which the quilter and her friends sat stitching. The plain lines could be marked easily, even as the quilt was stretched in the frame. The last reason for plain quilting was that quilters who quilted a lot knew that they would better apply their fancy designs where they would show and be admired—in alternate plain blocks, in sashing

2. Hanging Diamond. Plain quilting used on an appliqué block.

between the blocks, and on the borders. So I hope as you are considering your quilt top, you will be mentally X-ing out some areas of the quilt for plain quilting while reserving the open areas for fancy designs.

Now that you've cleared away some of the quilt top, you can get down to the "fun" part—choosing the fancy patterns. When looking for block designs, choose a pattern that fits at least 1/2 inch in from the seams of the block. You want the design to be framed by the block, not melt into the little shadow line of the seam. After choosing your pattern, consider doing filler quilting up to the edges of it, perhaps extending the lines of quilting from the pieced blocks into the plain area. (See Illustration 3) But, you say, isn't that an awful lot of quilting? Won't I be just as well off with less of this plain line stuff? The answer is...maybe. If what you need is a quilt done quickly or one that will hold up to five or so years of wear, it is your choice to do minimal quilting. But I have a hunch that since you are reading this book, you are interested in making your quilts as beautiful and lasting as old-time quilters did. I have often seen an antique tattered quilt, a hundred or more years old, held together only by the wealth of handquilting stitches in it. Assuming that you are interested in making quilts that last (all modern battings aside), please keep in mind that your quilting will be the framework of the piece. Build your quilt well with more, not less, quilting.

As you choose quilting designs for your borders, you face a few more choices. One large border is an ideal area for a flowing fancy design such as a cable or feather plume. Again choose a pattern which fits the border, leaving at least 1/2 inch in from the interior blocks of the quilt and at least 3/4 of an inch from the outside edge. Remember your quilt is not yet bound, and the binding will cover the border at least a quarter inch. It is often helpful to mark dashes, the middle line of your border so that you can place the design exactly down the middle. If your quilt has two borders, you may choose a large pattern that weaves across both borders. That is a "trick" many Amish quilters used. It is most helpful in unifying the overall look of your quilt and subtly coordinating even dramatically different colored borders. When you start to mark your borders, you usually start with the corners first and mark out to the midpoint (half-way mark) of your borders in an "L" fashion. This automatically makes any fitting (or fudging) occur at the middle of your borders—not at the much more conspicuous corners. Speaking of the midpoint of your borders, before you panic about making the pattern fit, the midpoint is the perfect place to mark a block-type pattern and create a new area of interest (and incidentally turn a negative into a positive.) Consider a round or oval wreath kind of pattern. That could be where you date and dedicate your quilt and you'll have four chances—at all the midpoints—to personalize your quilt. It will not be too obvious a signature but one which coordinates with your overall quilting theme. (See Illustration 4)

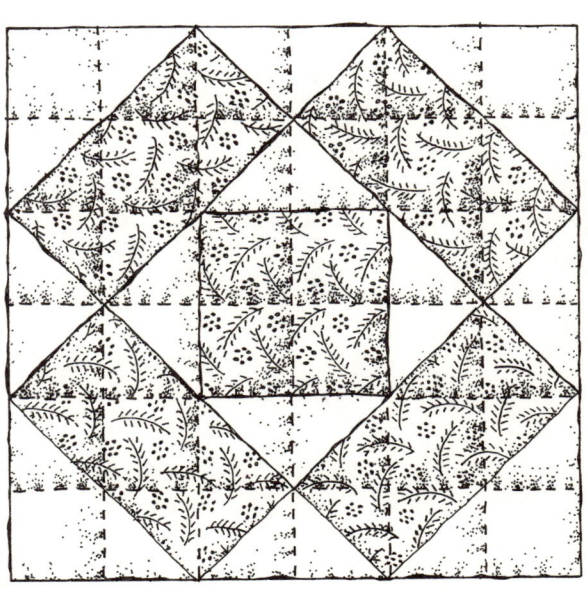

1. Crosshatching. Plain quilting used over a pieced block.

If you're determined you want your border markings to meet smoothly, their joining, at the most, is only as long as one repeat of the pattern. The repeat of the border pattern means the measurement of the pattern as it repeats, i.e. curves up and down. A compact design such as the border on page 24 has a small repeat only 3¼ inches long. A larger border pattern, like the cable and feather on pages 46 and 47, has a repeat 9 inches long. That is all you have to fit—or fudge. And it is usually better to stretch the bridge, making a slightly longer cable curve for instance, than to jam up the design. To get a feeling for how different quilters handle the joining of their border patterns, take a little time to study photographs of antique quilts, particularly Amish quilts. The Quilt Engagement Calendars offer many such examples.

If the idea of making patterns meet and marking corners scares you, you can always drop back to Amish Border Solution B—just run the pattern straight across the borders from edge to edge. (See p. 59) Perfectly acceptable.

Perhaps your quilt is an appliqué piece and the blocks meet without sashing. At that cross of seams, choose a block pattern which will cover and distract the viewer's eye from the seams. You want the viewer to be primarily impressed with your appliqué, not the construction of the background blocks.

Although these directions may not answer immediately all your questions before you actually start to mark your quilt top, as you mark you will likely work out your problems as they occur or Eureka!—you'll have chosen a pattern that fits without any on-the-job adjustments. But because there may be adjustments, please use quilt markers—pencils, chalk markers, soapstone, etc.—that can be erased or rubbed out if you are dissatisfied with your markings. The bad news is that there hasn't yet been invented the "perfect" quilt-marking tool. I know

3. A fancy quilting pattern complimented by plain quilting pattern, with filler quilting extended up to it.

Lastly, in choosing your quilting patterns, think of what the back of your quilt will look like. That was a vital consideration for an old-time quilter. Since quilts were often washed only once a year, usually in the spring after the daily use of the quilt in the cold months of the year, the quilter would turn over her quilt as it became soiled. A quilt is a two-sided piece and ideally should be as beautiful from the back as from the front. I have seen a lot of quilts from the back as I judged quilt shows. Too often the placement of the quilting patterns reminded me of potato prints stamped on the fabric—isolated designs with large puffs of batting between. A quilt reinforced and unified with filler quilting does not have this amateurish look—it seems complete, well-made, and harmonious to the eye. Give yourself a pat on the back if you are as proud of the back of your quilt as you are of the top. You have done a good job of marking.

of no such marker that makes a distinct line, stays on the quilt through all the handling we give it as we stitch, and then presto disappears as soon as we quilt the design or is guaranteed to wash out with the quilt's first bath. The good news is that with an erasable, rub-out-able marker, you can adjust and change the patterns as you mark—before even one stitch is committed to the quilt. I for one much prefer occasionally re-marking to the disaster of a marker that won't go away.

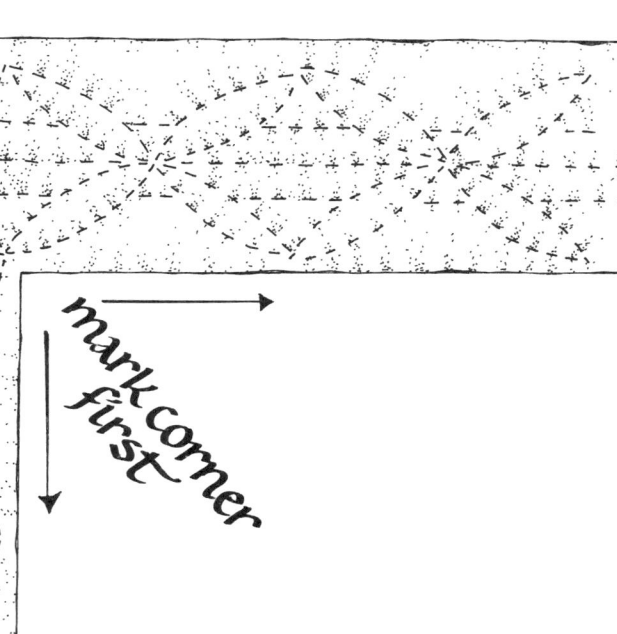

mark corner first

4. A border design marked from the corners outward and a different design placed at the midpoint (half-way mark) of the border. Initials can be quilted in the new design to personalize your quilt.

Univerjat Quilts

These first designs, seven in number, were drawn from two antique quilts that I now own. The first quilt, a very tattered Carolina Lily, in red, green, yellow and white, did not immediately get my attention. I was at an antique show, busily burrowing my way through a stack of quilts, and as I moved the Carolina Lily over to get to a more exciting piece, I noticed how heavy the quilt was—too heavy for how fragile and worn it appeared at first glance. I held it up to the light and the antique dealer helped me unfold the quilt. As I searched for the alternate white squares between the Lily blocks, a fantastic jungle of floral quilting designs emerged. No wonder the quilt weighed so much—it had as much thread in it as it did fabric! As I traced the quilting stitches on the border and came to a vainglorious rooster perched on a vine crowded with strange fruits and flowers, I realized the quiltmaker had been an artist. These are happy, freely drawn designs and evidently the quilter let her imagination run wild as she marked her quilt top. So I did some fancy funds-juggling and bought the quilt. I immediately put it on the bed and am happy to say that the old Carolina Lily quilt "dreams good."

The second quilt came as a bonus. I received a letter from the antique dealer reporting she had acquired another quilt from the same family. A Rose of Sharon appliqué, the quilt was made in similar fabrics and colors. Both date from around 1865-1890. The family name was Univerjat and both quilts were made in Michigan. To Shirley Raleigh of Denley's Antiques, St. Clair Shores, Michigan—thanks for the lay-away.

Embellished star—for a 10½-inch square.

Both these designs fit an 8-inch square.

This elaborate 11-inch border design continues on to the next page. It reminds me of English crewel embroidery. Place the pattern so that the rooster is at the midpoint of the border (half-way mark) and draw the pattern out to the corners.

No special way to get around the corners. The design just ran out to the edge of the quilt and picked up again at right angles.

a. Primitive vase design. For an 8-inch block or repeated, as in the source quilt, along an 8-inch border.

b. This design duplicated one of the appliqué patterns. For a 10½-inch square.

A unique solution to a round feather wreath on a square block. Fits a 12-inch block.

Lancaster County Stencils

I bought these hand-made quilt stencils at a quilt show in Michigan—although the dealer had gotten them years before in Lancaster County, Pennsylvania. Judging from the paper they were cut from, I estimate their date as being around 1900-1925.

a. Little hearts in a ring—for an 8-inch square.

b. Birdie—probably used in combination with other designs. Nicely fits a 5-inch half-block (Courtesy of Julie Brown, Flushing, Michigan).

A quilted valentine for a 13-inch square. This design would make a lovely pillow top or the center of an all-white christening quilt.

a. Pot of flowers for a 10-inch square.

b. Obviously the first cousin to the bird in the valentine on page 15. For a 10-inch square, or when marked on the diagonal, fits an 8-inch square.

This elaborate design has an Art Nouveau feeling. Repeated in an 11-inch border or in a 16-inch block.

The Miller Auction Boxes

One cold April morning, I stood in the yard of an Amish farmhouse—along with about two hundred other freezing souls. I pulled my shawl around my head, rubbed my rapidly numbing hands together, and wondered what on earth I was doing there, at such an early hour and in such a wind. Then I noticed a knot of Amish ladies gathered around the bedsteads which had been set on the front lawn. I wandered over and started examining the linens—all manner of sheets, rugs, quilts, blankets and afghans were piled on the bare mattresses. Among these jumbled furnishings, I found a treasure—three boxes of handmade quilt stencils. I was so excited! I had dismissed all hope of obtaining one of the quilts—there were "heavy-hitting" quilt dealers in the crowd—but the stencils... maybe, just maybe, I could buy them.

So I waited—for hours—as the tools, dishes, furniture, even the house and the land were sold to the highest bidder. To keep warm, I consoled myself with coffee, doughnuts, pie, sandwiches, and chili soup (you eat well at an Amish auction.)

As the quilts came up for bid, I greedily watched "my boxes." It was now evident who had come for the quilts and the bidding was entirely out of my range. When the auctioneer lifted the boxes up and began the bidding, I had several competitors, but one by one, they "got off" the boxes and finally the auctioneer said "Sold!"—and pointed to me! I wanted to whoop and jump around, but seeing as how such a display of elation seemed out of place in that crowd, I just gathered up my booty and went to pay the auctioneer's assistant—quickly.

Later I found out my friend Rebecca Haarer had spread the word that I wanted the stencils for a book on quilting patterns. So now I knew why one of the quilt dealers had winked at me and said, "Next time, no mercy!"

The designs are from the Joe and Anne E. Miller family of Middlebury, Indiana. Some of the patterns looked quite old—pre-1900—but others could be as recent as the 1960's.

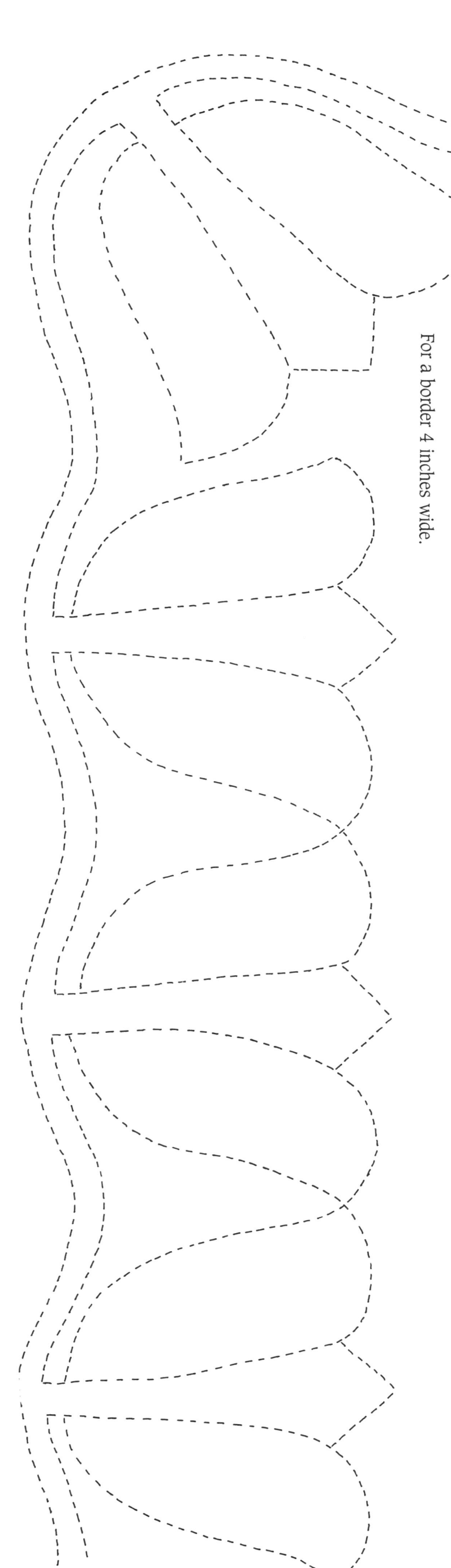

For a border 4 inches wide.

a. A delicate leaf design for a 9-inch block.

b. The mate to Design a.—for a border 2½ inches wide.

c. For a 7-inch square.

A feather variation for a 13-inch block.

b. An interesting feather corner for a 4-inch border or a 10-inch half-block.

a. This design resembles a saw blade. For a 9½-inch block.

Repeated as a 5-inch border.

a. Repeated as a 6-inch border.

b. For a 4-inch border.

a. A pumpkin seed border 3-inches wide.

b. Hex-like star design for a 10-inch block.

Hearts repeated as a 6-inch border.

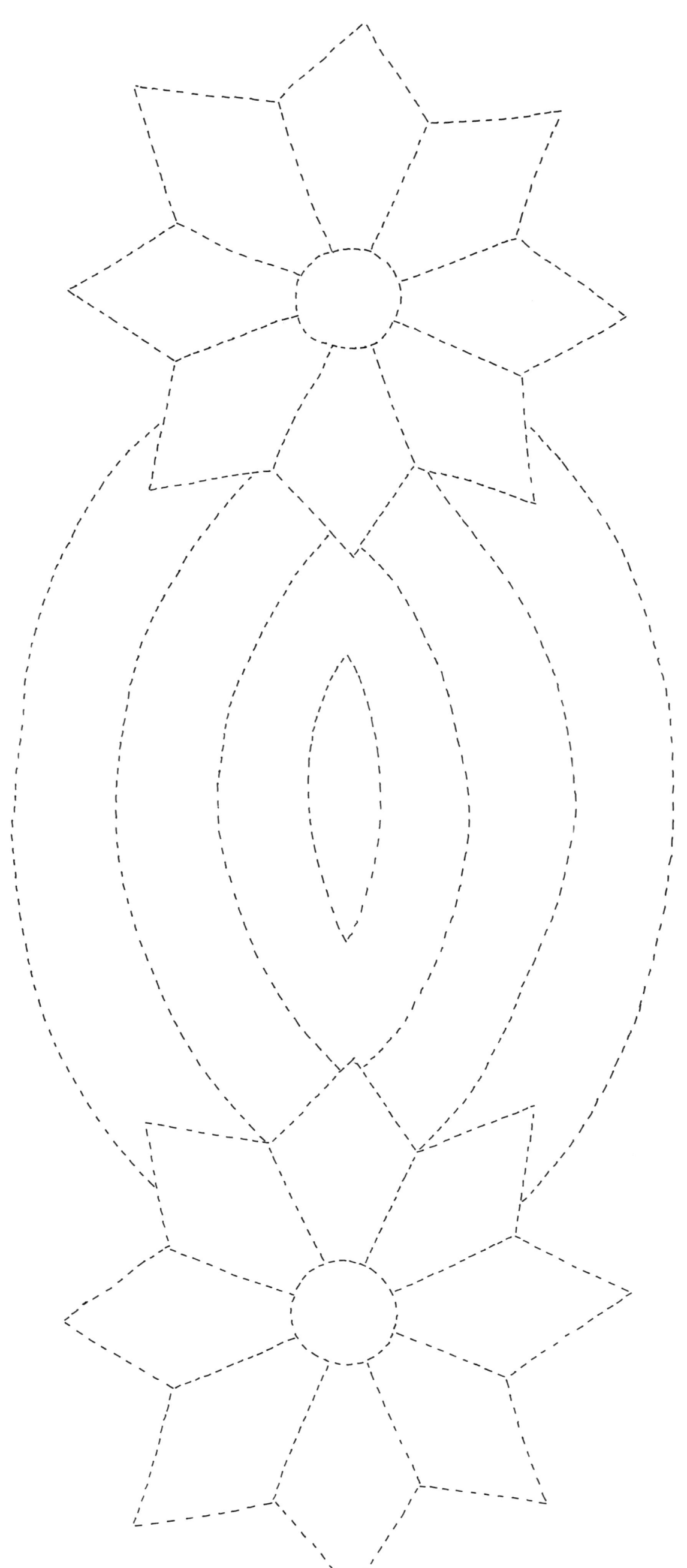

This design looks like a combination of a cable and a Dresden Plate pattern. For a 7-inch border.

a. Little tulips swinging in a ring. Fits a 7-inch square.

b. One of the more unusual Amish patterns I have seen, especially with the four heavy-footed little birds around the outside of the main tulip design. For a 10-inch block.

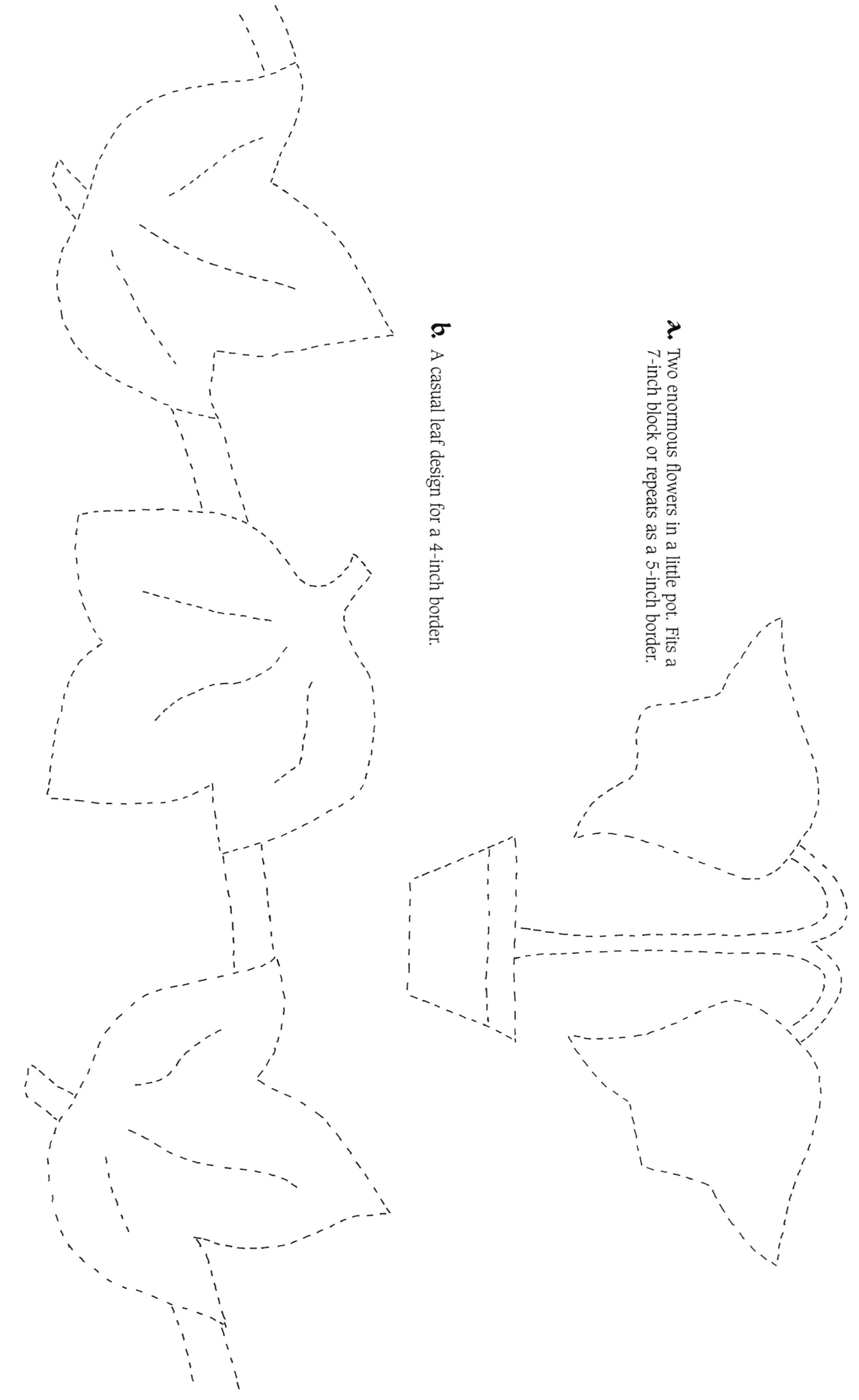

a. Two enormous flowers in a little pot. Fits a 7-inch block or repeats as a 5-inch border.

b. A casual leaf design for a 4-inch border.

a. A design of hearts for a 6-inch square.

b. Perhaps this complex flower was inspired by an embroidery pattern. Fits a 9½-inch block.

Carrow & McNerney

These little designs are from the same antique quilt. Presently owned by Carrow-McNerney Country Antiques, the source was a fragile Ohio Star quilt, pieced in indigo, red, and white. Carefully petti-pointed smack in the center of the quilt was this proud inscription: "Made by Harriet Lovisa Youngs, Age 22, S. Venice, N.Y., 1847."

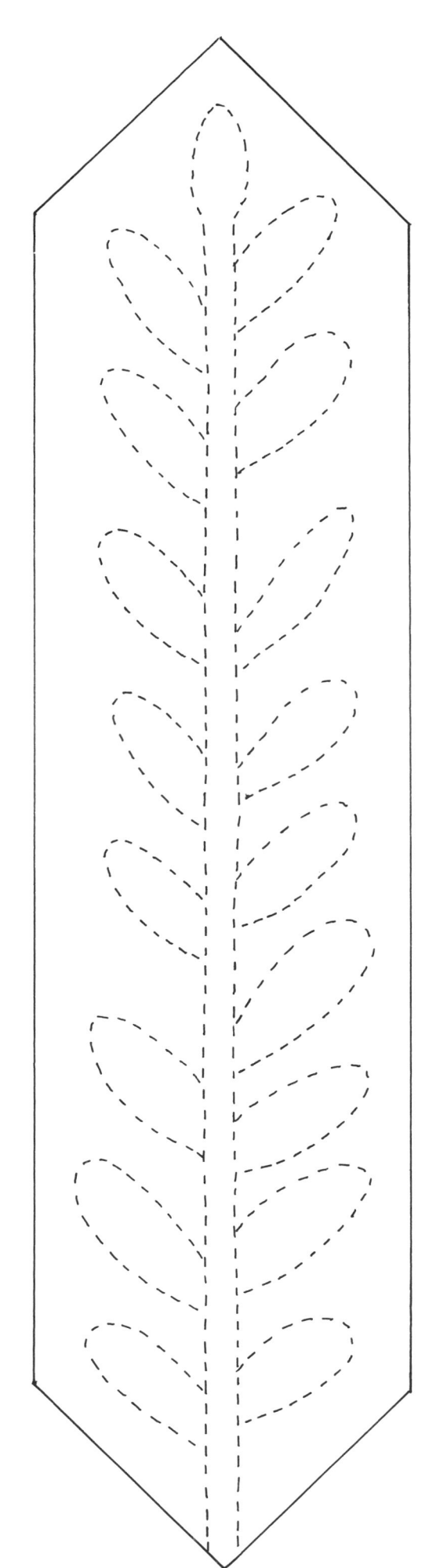

Michigan Historical Museum

The following designs were all drawn from the same quilt which is now in the Michigan Historical Museum in Lansing, Michigan. The quilt is the Old Maid's Puzzle, pieced in lovely soft green, blue, pink, and brown calicoes. The quilt is set with alternate plain white blocks and surrounded on all sides with a Wild Goose Chase border. It has a well-documented history and amply illustrates how precious a quilt can be, both as an emotional touchstone for its maker and her descendants, and as historical artifact for us.

The quilt was probably made around 1854 at a quilting party in Stanley Corners, New York. Each quilter was invited to bring her favorite quilting pattern to mark in the white blocks. Sometime before 1860, the quilt was given to Ellen Throckmorton-Baker, who took it with her as she and her husband, Lorenzo Adelbert Baker, and her young daughter, Mary Elizabeth, moved west to the "wilderness"—that new state of Michigan. In 1862, Mr. Baker volunteered for service and until the end of the Civil War, fought in the Michigan 50th Regiment of Engineers. Fortunately, he came home to his family in 1865. Meanwhile little Mary was growing up and in 1879, when she was thirty years old, Mary married Dr. Louis DeLamarter who practiced medicine only five blocks south of the capitol building in Lansing. Mary became the caretaker of her mother's prized quilt and well understood its importance. She kept it clean and often pointed out to her daughter, Louella, the beautiful stitching in the quilt.

In a letter written when she was 85 years old, Mary addressed these words to her daughter, now Mrs. Edward Dawson, who had moved to New York City.

The special topic of this letter is **The Quilt**. *It begins to oppress my mind. I have only a few treasures to bestow…Now and then I show the quilt to someone and have been noticing the various reactions. To my surprise appreciation does not often abide where I expected it.*

The quilt is really a treasure for its **quilting**. *In that respect it is a sample of what was one of the fine arts of the previous century…I find it difficult to allow that quilt to go where it would be a common thing…After I am gone I would like it to go where it would be appreciated as a specimen of lost art.*

—March 31, 1936

This feather loop was quilted in the tiniest stitches—11 to the inch. Clearly the work of an expert needlewoman. This pattern, and the one of page 25 were obviously stitched by the same hand. Mentally, I labelled the unknown quilter The Show Off since her work was conspicuously placed in the center of the quilt! For an 8-inch block.

Louella Dawson took her mother's letter to heart when she became the owner of the precious family quilt. In 1960, she wrote the State Museum in Lansing, asking if they were interested in the quilt for their collection. Of course, the Museum was delighted to accept the quilt and once more, the Old Maid's Puzzle quilt, carefully preserved by three generations of women, travelled again from New York to Michigan. This time the quilt came by Rail Express, rather than the rougher journey it had made by oxcart in the previous century.

The quilt was exhibited to the public in the State Museum in 1984. I went to that exhibit and remembered the fine antique Old Maid's Puzzle and its beautiful quilting patterns. When I was researching designs, I naturally went to the museum and asked for permission to copy the patterns for this book. As I opened the file on Artifact #SM-1038-54, I found Mrs. DeLamarter's letter and was very moved as I read of her longing to preserve her quilt for future generations. I have to think that Ellen Baker, Mary DeLamarter, and Louella Dawson would be happy to see these patterns presented here, and to know that quilting, far from being the "lost art" referred to in the letter of 1936, is being revived, practiced, and appreciated once again all over the world.

a. Quarter feather circles for an 8-inch block.

b. For an 8-inch block.

b. This design is similar to the half-block on p. 32. Fits an 8-inch block.

a. Notice the outline around the design which almost gives a corded effect. This extra effort gives a sophistication to an otherwise simple pattern. For an 8-inch square.

This pattern is a nice combination of a few feather shapes and plain-line quilting. Used as you see it here, it fits an 11-inch block. Tilted 90° it fits very snugly in 8 inches.

Another pattern quilted by The Show Off in her 11-stitches-to-the-inch style. Actually my drawing shows stitches larger than her work! For an 8-inch square.

Shipshe Auction Quilt

This design was drawn from an antique quilt, a Corn and Beans pattern, made about 1900. The indigo and white quilt had seen hard use and only the handstitching held it together. I was admiring the quilting design when it was snatched up by the auctioneer at the Shipshe Auction (held every Wednesday in Shipshewana, Indiana) and sold to the highest bidder. Anxiously I followed the quilt as it travelled through the crowd to its new owner. The man was a little bewildered as I asked permission to sketch the pattern, but he graciously helped me spread out the quilt over the top of an old wringer washer. I quickly drew the pattern and handed the quilt back to him. Good thing I always carry a pen and an old envelope to jot down things on! For a 10-inch block.

The Riddle Tulip

The title refers to the last name of the owners of this quilt, because there is nothing puzzling about this straightforward tulip design. Repeated in a 9-inch border.

Playing with Patterns

Many quiltmakers avidly collect whole dictionaries of quilting patterns. Yet when we complete a new quilt top, we leaf through our books and the designs seem too familiar, too average for our latest creation. Maybe what we could use is a new outlook—more precisely, an outlook 90° different from the straight-on way you are presently looking at these pages. Turn to any page of this book that has block patterns, push the book away from you 90° on the right (a quarter turn). The block designs formerly set square on the page now appear "on point." It's a trick to make a design cover more area (i.e. fit a larger block). The design on p. 35 (for an 8-inch square) when viewed at that 90° angle, will fit a 10-inch block (A). Old-time quilters were familiar with the block-on-point method and often used it when designing their quilt tops. They didn't have to piece as many blocks that way! A few designs intended for blocks go nicely on lattice strips between quilt squares (B). As you discover designs in this book that look interesting "on point," mark a pencil "X" next to them. Now these designs can do double duty for you in different size blocks. And there are more ways to play with patterns...

a. This classic heart design shown on p. 35 fits an 8-inch square, but turned "on point"—as seen here—it nicely fills a 10-inch block.

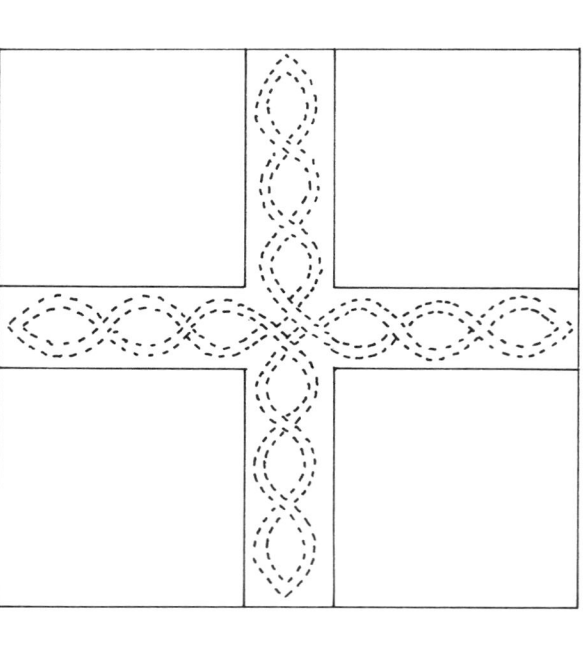

b. Originally designed for a block, this cable variation from p. 53 will fit a 2½ - 3-inch lattice strip.

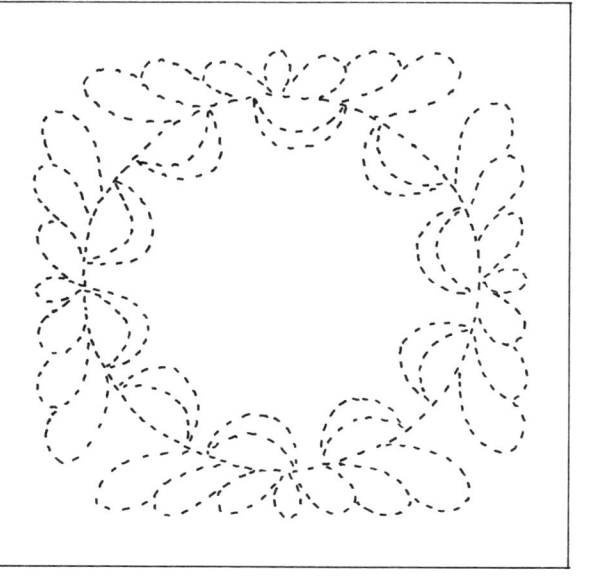

c. From p. 42, a feather wreath you can use without the original center design.

"Drops and Adds" is a term I use to describe another way to stretch your design possibilities. When you "drop" (don't use) part of a design, you reduce its size or you simplify the pattern. Take a few pieces of white typing paper folded double (for no show-through) and cover up parts of the designs with the paper. You can "erase" the middle of a block (C) or cut a pattern in half or quarters to fit half-blocks and corners (D and E). Conversely you can add elements to the designs or combine two patterns (F) in one. A row or two of simple echo quilting around the outside of a design will seem to make it "blossom." (G) Other straight lines—use a ruler here—will extend the pattern to the corners of the block. (H)

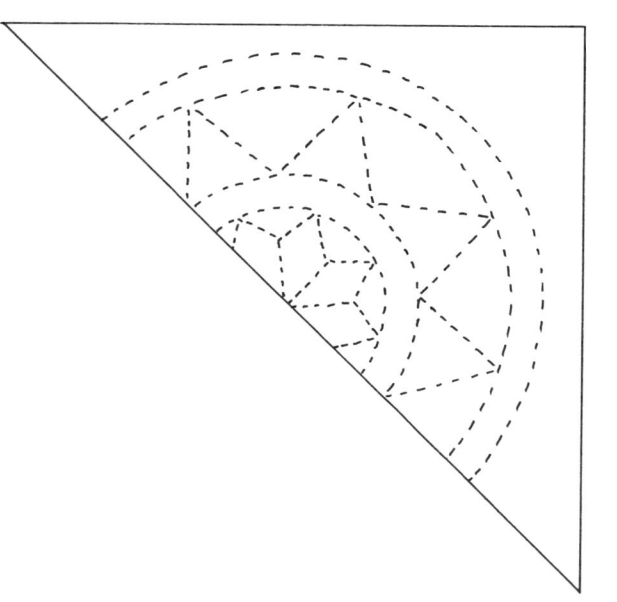

d. An old-timey star hex, from p. 24, becomes a rising sun on a half-block.

j. The tiny flower from p. 44 can be repeated in an L-shape for a border and corner.

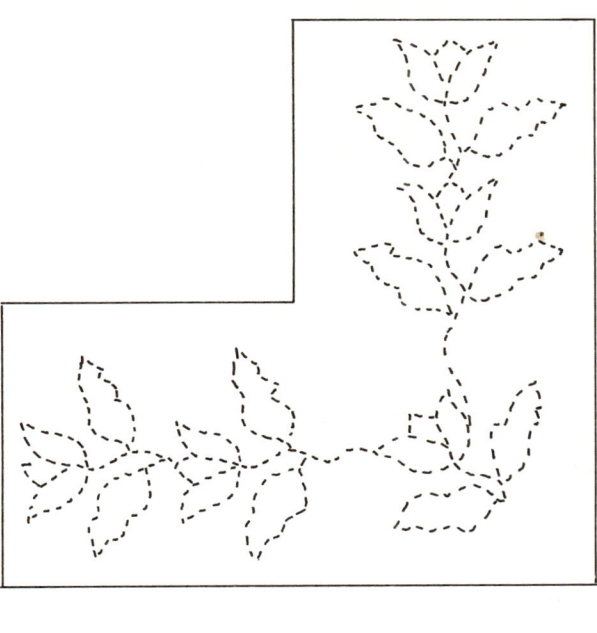

h. The addition of straight lines marked with a ruler enlarges and pulls the design toward the corners of the square. (Design from p. 21)

i. This corner design (p. 21) can be multiplied four times to form an elegant feather pattern for a large block.

Then there is the "divide and multiply" method. First you take a part of design you like (divide) and then repeat it (multiply) several times in a block. It is easy to see how your new design will look if you cut a square of tracing paper the size of your quilt block and fold it in a cross and in an X. Put the tracing paper over the part of the design you like, trace it, and using the creases as guidelines, repeat it evenly around the square. (I) If you multiply a design in a straight line (an L-shaped piece of tracing paper used here) you have a new border pattern. (J)

If all of this is beginning to sound like quilt math—90° angles, drops and adds, divide and multiply—don't get upset. Get excited instead! Playing with patterns is time well spent and only requires an open mind, some tracing paper, and a pencil. Soon you will find your dictionary of patterns has expanded into an encyclopedia of quilting possibilities.

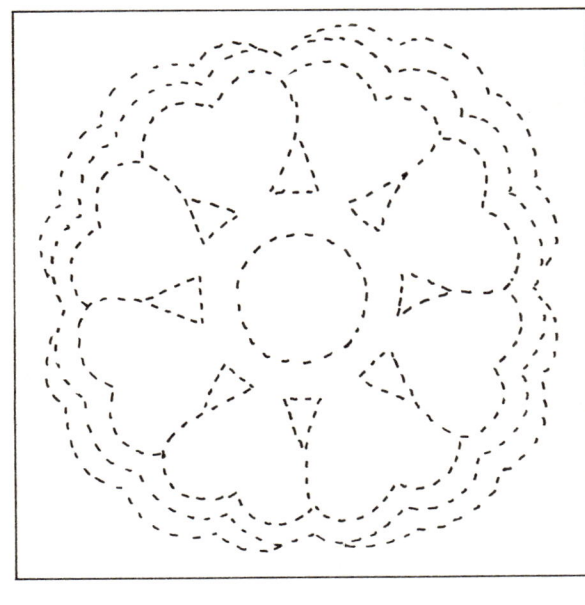

g. Little hearts in a ring (p. 14) seems to blossom when lines of echo quilting are added.

e. One quarter of the design from p. 32.

f. Little star in a big star, combination of designs from p. 7 and p. 62.

Fisher Quilt

The source quilt for these two designs was a primitive Flowers in a Vase appliqué. (I use the term primitive only to describe the folk-y feeling of the design, not its execution.) Large blooms of red, gold, and green seemed to spring out of the quilt and the overall impact was so great that unless the quilt was handled—the weight of it felt—the thousands of stitches might have remained undiscovered. Where four of the large appliqué blocks came together, the sunflower design was quilted. It was so skillfully executed that one really had to concentrate to pick out the actual seams of the block.

The quilt was probably made in northern Indiana just prior to the Civil War. The sunflower fits an 11-inch square.

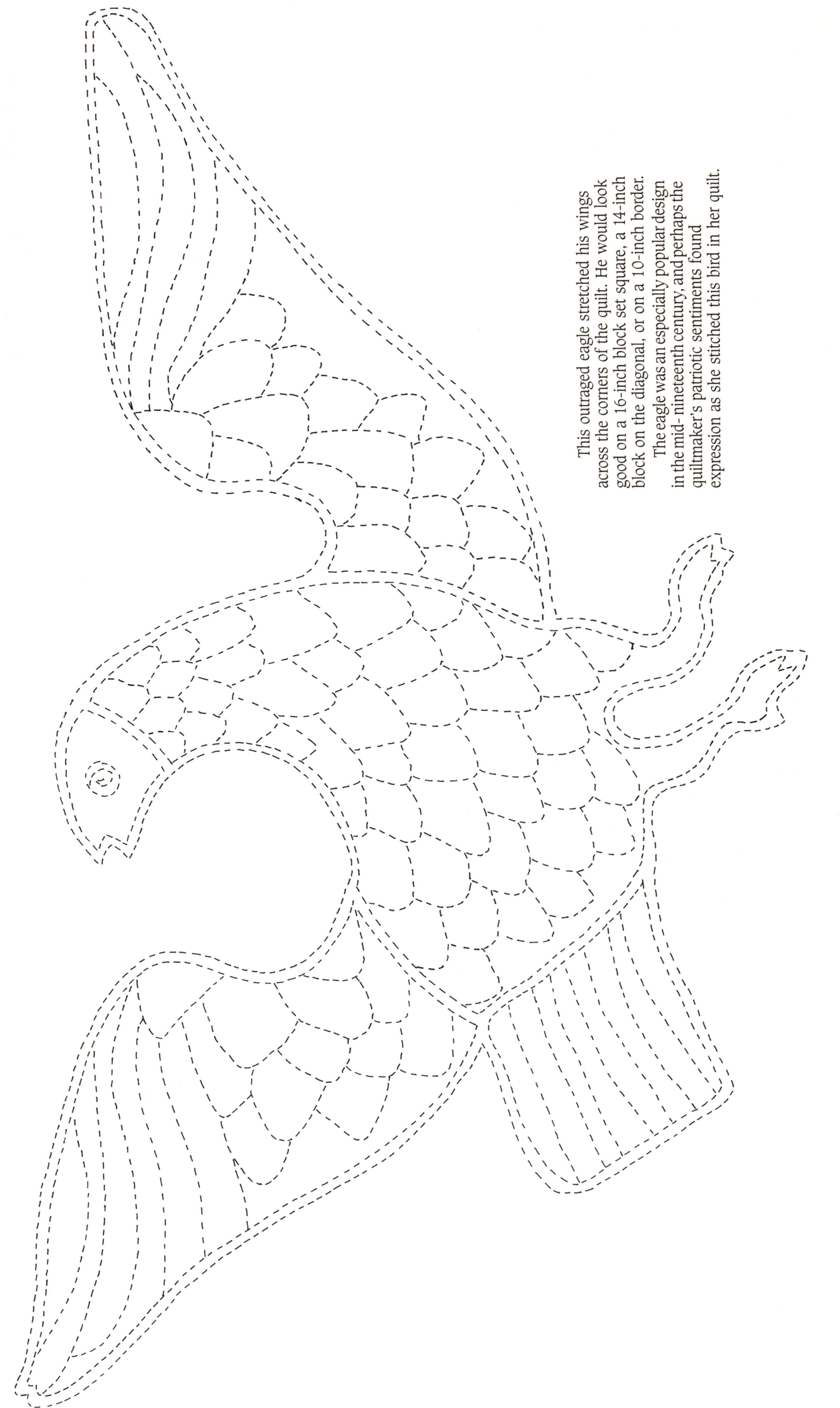

This outraged eagle stretched his wings across the corners of the quilt. He would look good on a 16-inch block set square, a 14-inch block on the diagonal, or on a 10-inch border.

The eagle was an especially popular design in the mid-nineteenth century, and perhaps the quiltmaker's patriotic sentiments found expression as she stitched this bird in her quilt.

Silber/Ruether

The designs on these pages are courtesy of Julie Silber and Linda Ruether. These partners owned a store, Mary Strickler's Quilt, which was one of the first quilt shops in the United States. The fine antique quilts which came from Mary Strickler's Quilt helped spread the "gospel of quilt"—that is, that quilts might be functional craft objects but they are also the most accessible historical works of women's art.

These designs are from the same quilt—a pieced Sunburst in brilliant red, green, and orange. The feather circle fits a 9½-inch square and the little tree with swirls was for a 9½-inch half-block. The inscription on this quilt is quite specific. In one half-block is quilted "July 28, 1844" and another states "1847, made by Margaret L. R. Wilker, her quilt." It is not surprising that this masterpiece of piecing and handquilting was three years in the making!

Julie and Linda have continued their involvement in the "quilt world" even though Mary Strickler's Quilt, as a retail store, has closed. They sell antique quilts, organize quilt exhibitions, lecture, write, and recently are concerned with producing films about quilts and the women who made them. At present, Julie Silber is the curator of the Esprit De Corp collection of extraordinary Amish quilts. The quilts hang everywhere at the Esprit headquarters, serving as inspiration to the fabric/clothing designers who work there. And at the same time, quilters, like pilgrims to Mecca, come and wander through the halls of Esprit. It is very comforting to me to know that the magenta Esprit shirt I bought years ago might be the "offspring" of an Amish quilt!

This tulip spray is a graceful design for a border 8 inches wide. Or you can use it as in the original—repeated down the length of the wide stripes of an Amish Bars quilt. Made of black and maroon wool, the quilt is dated 1892 and its origin is Lancaster County, Pennsylvania.

Ruby Hostetler

The evening I came to Mrs. Ruby Hostetler's house, our visit was supposed to last about an hour. But you know how it is when two quilters start talking and swapping patterns...about four hours later, we finally unscrambled our drawings—they were all over the table and floor—and parted with the promise we would write each other.

The basement of the Hostetler home is set up to accommodate Mrs. Hostetler's quilting patterns, neatly filed in boxes and hanging from nails on the wall. A large table, lit from above, is her drawing space as she designs patterns and marks quilt tops. She and I both agreed that too many quilters are "scared" of border corners and of making designs meet. All her border designs have tackled that problem and meet beautifully. Although these designs are not exactly antique, I knew you would enjoy these patterns from the collection of a master quilt marker.

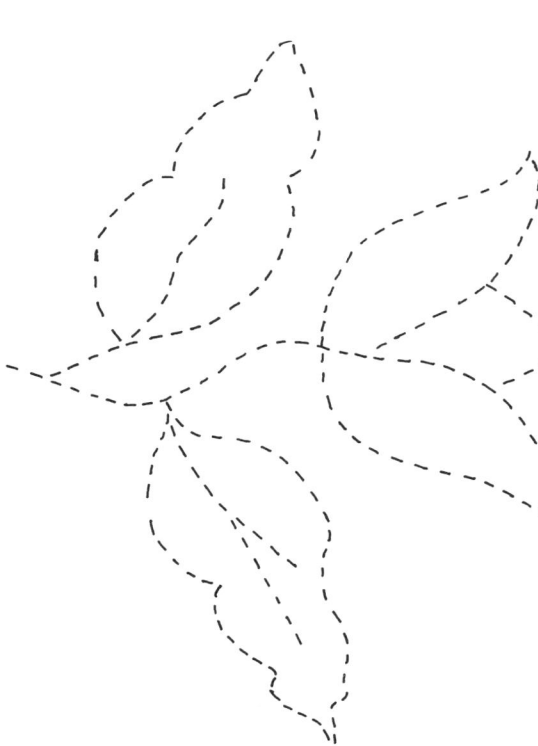

a. A little flower for a 4-inch square (drawn on the diagonal).

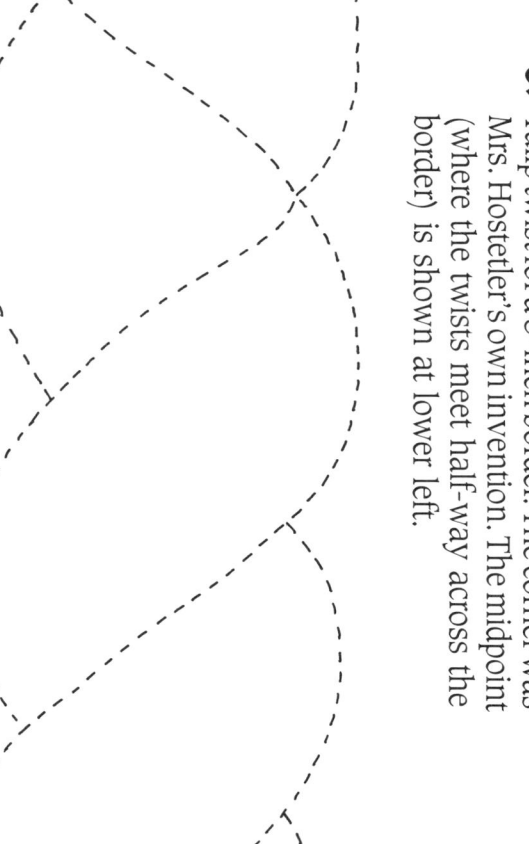

b. Tulip twist for a 3-inch border. The corner was Mrs. Hostetler's own invention. The midpoint (where the twists meet half-way across the border) is shown at lower left.

a.

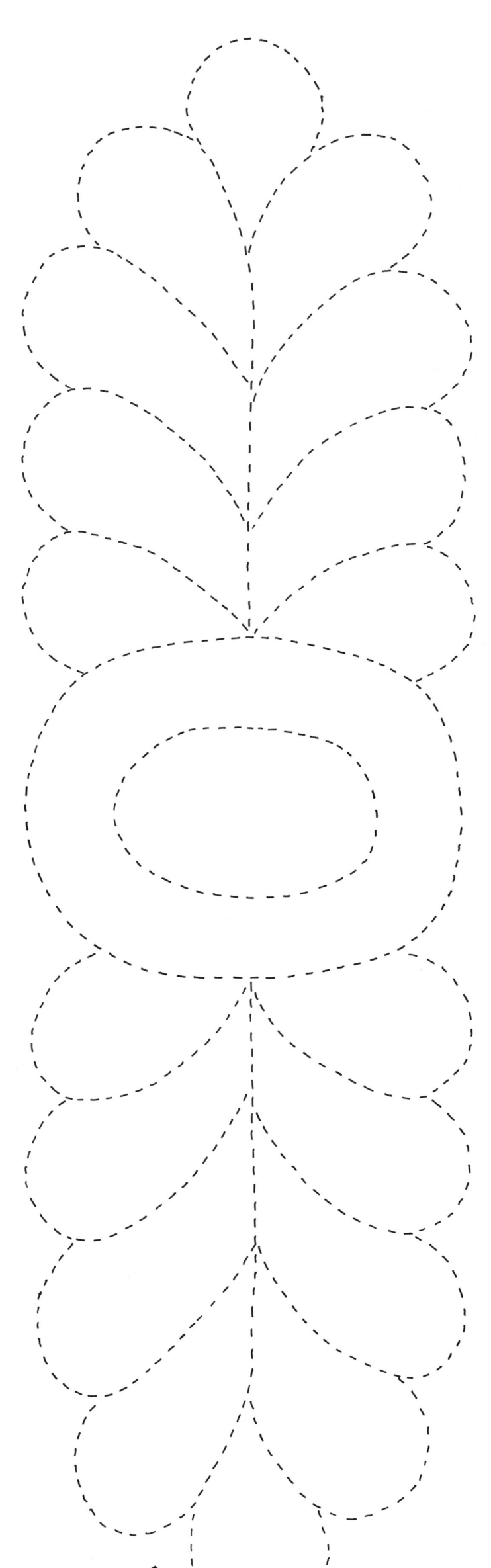
b.

These oval and feather designs fit 4½-inch lattice strips or borders.

A combination wave and plume pattern which winds gracefully around the border always going in the same direction. The "trick" to mark this is the bottom line which scallops around the design but is not attached to it. If you mark only this scallop first (corners first, then toward the midpoints) you have a preview of where the pattern joining will happen before you are committed to drawing the rest of the stencil. It makes elongating or shortening the design a lot easier. For an 8-inch border.

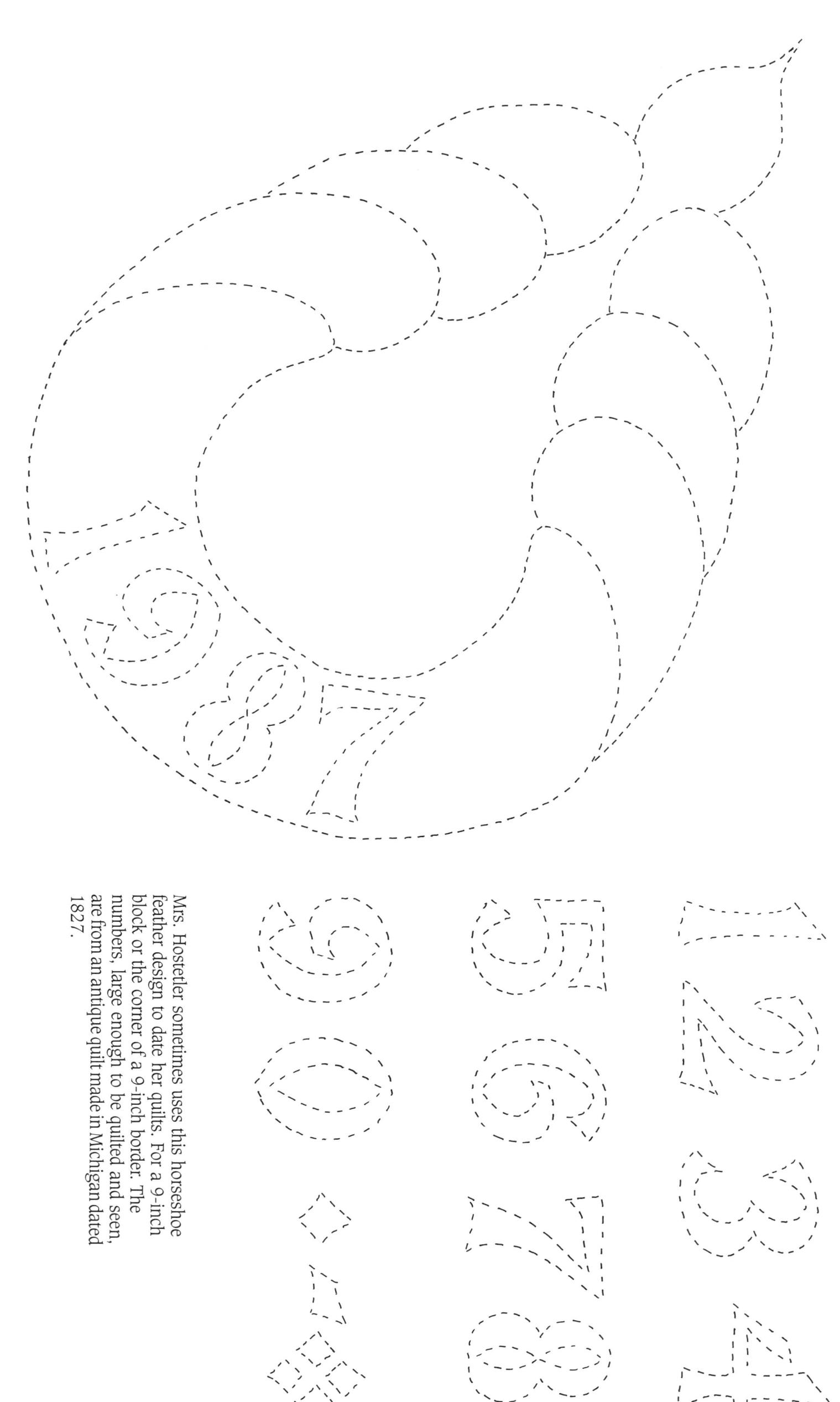

Mrs. Hostetler sometimes uses this horseshoe feather design to date her quilts. For a 9-inch block or the corner of a 9-inch border. The numbers, large enough to be quilted and seen, are from an antique quilt made in Michigan dated 1827.

The Yoder Sisters

An elaborate corner for a 7-inch border or perfect for 16-inch right triangles, like the large triangles around an Amish Center Diamond pattern.

I corresponded with the Yoder sisters, Minnie and Lydia, long before I ever met them. Since they are Amish and do not travel as freely as I do, I took the initiative to drive up to see them. But I was late for my appointment! Speeding down the country road, I almost missed the neat white farmhouse at the crest of the hill. What caught my eye were these two tiny ladies wrestling with an enormous ladder as a neighbor man, temporarily stranded on the porch roof, likewise struggled to put up a length of eavestrough. I turned into the lane and chickens and cats scooted to the backyard. I wasn't much help with the ladder. The Yoder sisters and their neighbor actually had the task down to a science, since every year it was necessary to take down the eavestroughs in the autumn and put them up again in the spring once the threat of ice and snow accumulation had passed. Reluctantly I refused the offer of a kitten as the three of us entered the cool kitchen. The neighbor departed and a friend stopped by to buy eggs. I spent a most enjoyable afternoon with Misses Minnie and Lydia Yoder. Over lemonade and cookies, we three did what we liked best—talked quilts and swapped patterns.

a. Single plume repeated for a 6-inch border.

b. Design for a 7-inch block.

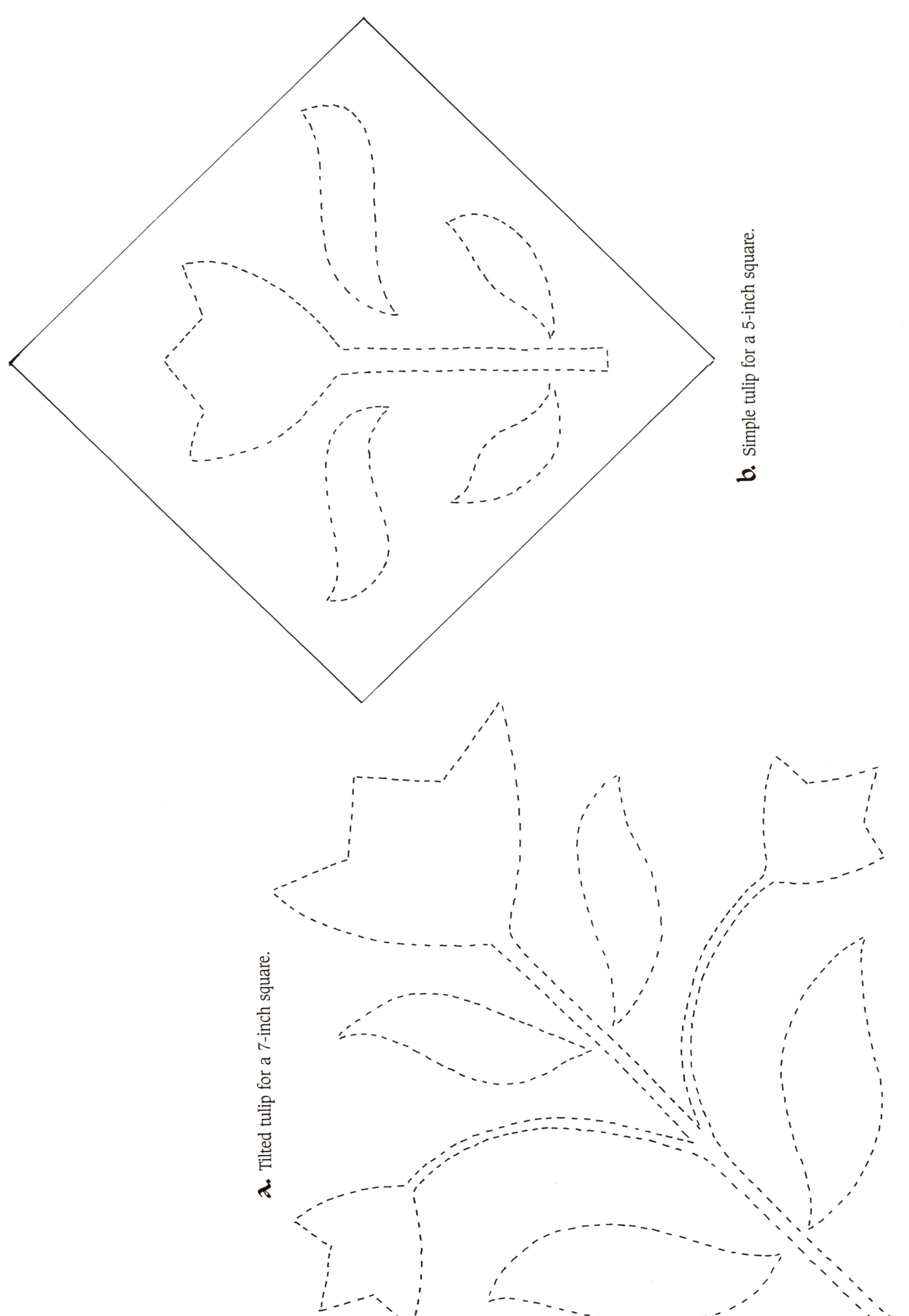

a. Tilted tulip for a 7-inch square.

b. Simple tulip for a 5-inch square.

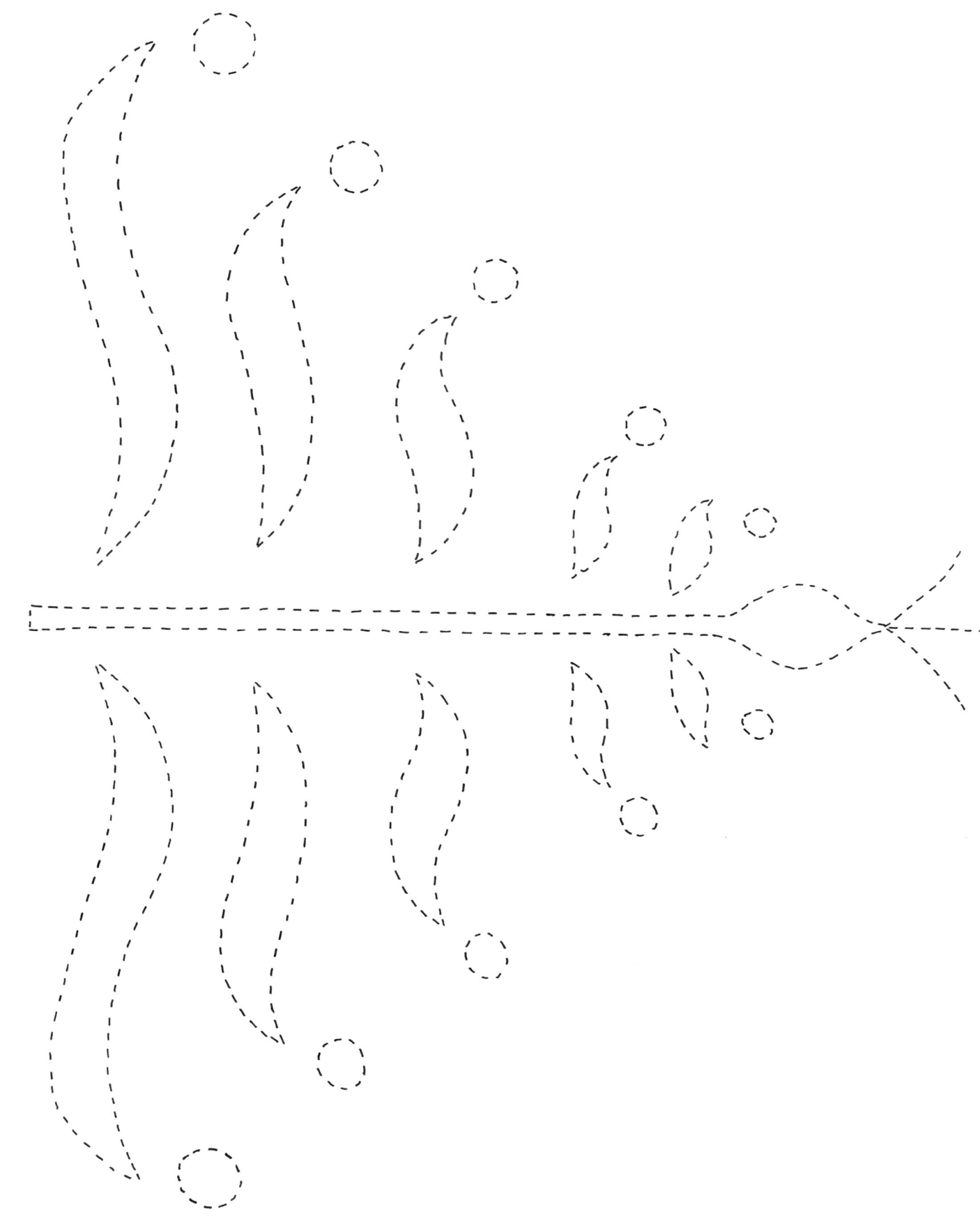

Old stencil for a 12-inch block. One of the sisters remarked, "I think it's a little Christmas tree."

The Pottinger Collection

An intertwined cable for a 9½-inch block.

In June of 1986, I had the privilege of spending two uninterrupted days collecting quilting designs from the quilts of David Pottinger's collection. The majority of the quilts were Amish quilts from the Mid-West, dating from the 1880's through the 1940's.

At first it was difficult to concentrate on the subtle handquilting designs, as I was distracted by the striking jewel-like colors and unique patchwork patterns. But as I handled more quilts and better focused my research, a thought took firm hold in my mind. My personal belief is that the most casual and simple part of the quiltmaking was the piecing of the top, and actually the handquilting—the tiny time-consuming stitches—was the most important feature of the quilt to the Amish quiltmaker herself. How else can one explain the minimal time (10-30 hours) spent piecing an average quilt top versus the 50-100 hours represented by the handquilting?

Our view of Amish quilts has been largely shaped by what we've seen in books or hanging on the walls of art galleries. Unfortunately the dark colors and fabrics (usually wool in the older quilts) prevent clear representation of the handquilting stitches in photographs. It is easy to be impressed with the graphic impact of an Amish quilt, even as we overlook what was probably the pride and joy for the quiltmaker—her unique quilting designs and the skillful, neat quilting stitches.

Another "clue" for me that handquilting was the most creative part of quiltmaking for the Amish quilter was that often, even on a very fine quilt, the backing was drawn up over the top, or a wide straight binding applied, then visibly machine stitched down. It seemed as if the "fun" part of quiltmaking having been completed, the maker was just eager to get her piece bound and on the bed!

This theory of mine—that handquilting was the most important aspect of quiltmaking to the Amish quilter—takes nothing away from the acknowledged beauty of Amish quilts. On the contrary, it can only deepen our appreciation of these lovely works of art. A final thought—if color and design is the soul of the Amish quilt, then handquilting is surely the heart.

Bird and branch for a 6-inch border. Found on a simple Star pattern quilt made by Anna W. Beechy Yoder for her son William. Made in 1940 in Emma, Indiana.

On Palm Sunday in 1964, a terrible tornado swept through northern Indiana. Homes and businesses were destroyed and many lives lost. As the survivors picked themselves up, relief packages of food, clothing, and bedding arrived from other Amish and Mennonite communities. When Olen and Irene Wingard opened their relief package from Pennsylvania, they found a classic Block and Diamond quilt. Pieced in soft grey and rose wool, the quilt dated from about 1900. This rose design was quilted in the triangles surrounding the center square. The original pattern was larger, for a 20-inch half-block. Reduced here because of size limitations, the rose fits a 15-inch half-block or a 10-inch border.

This 7-inch border pattern was drawn from a Log Cabin quilt made by Mrs. Henry (Susie) Miller from Topeka, Indiana sometime between 1910-1915.

a. The matching corner to the border on the facing page.

b. Folk art heart for a 6-inch block. From the effects of Mrs. Urias V. Yoder of Topeka, Indiana.

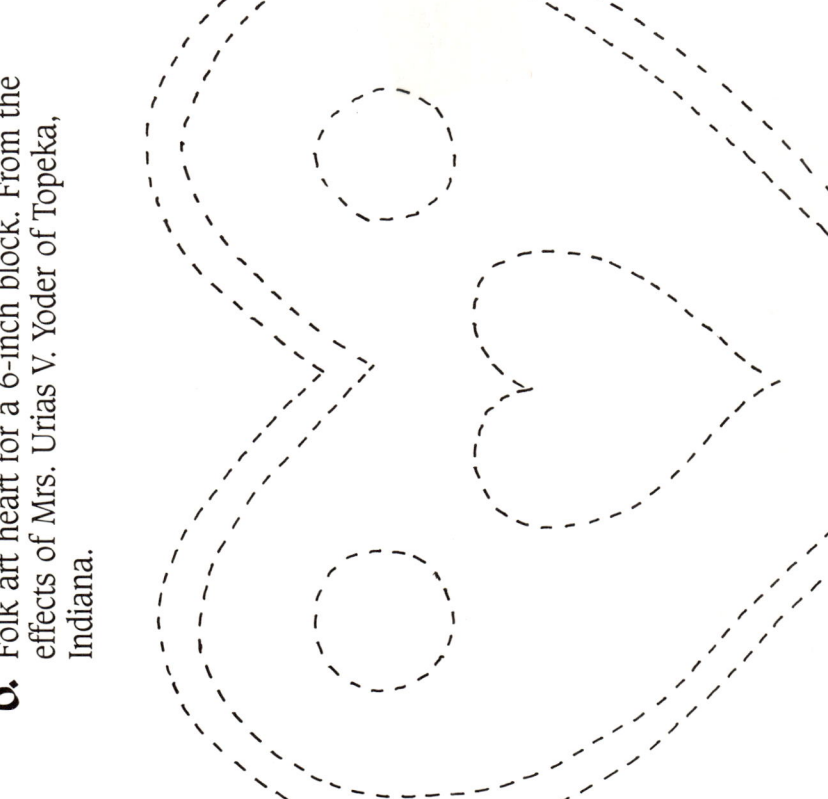

a. A 3-inch border inspired by the original block design.

b. Old stencil for an 8-inch block

Border design from a c. 1900 Baskets quilt. Perhaps it was a wedding quilt since it shows twin hearts. For a 6-inch border.

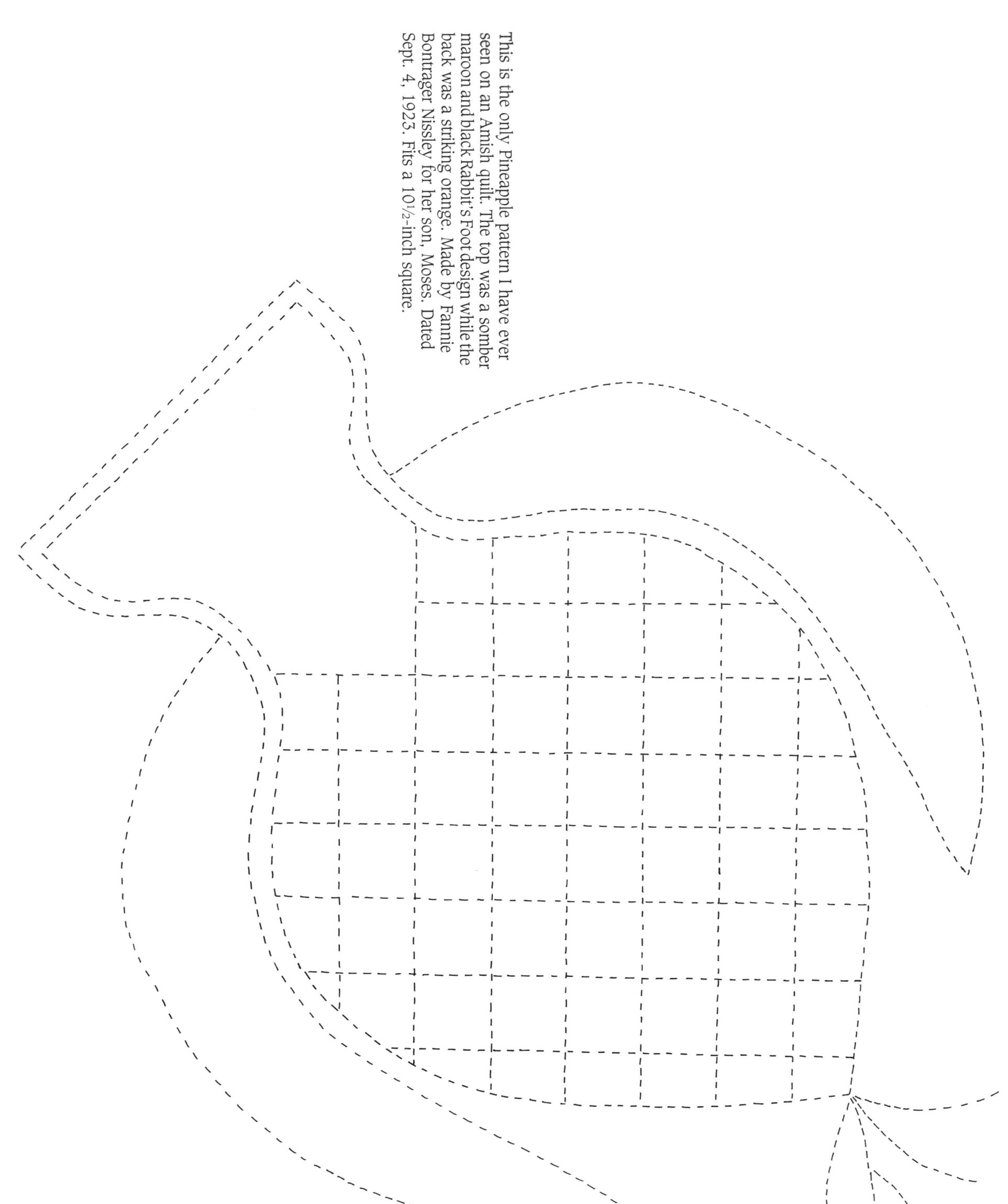

This is the only Pineapple pattern I have ever seen on an Amish quilt. The top was a somber maroon and black Rabbit's Foot design while the back was a striking orange. Made by Fannie Bontrager Nissley for her son, Moses. Dated Sept. 4, 1923. Fits a 10½-inch square.

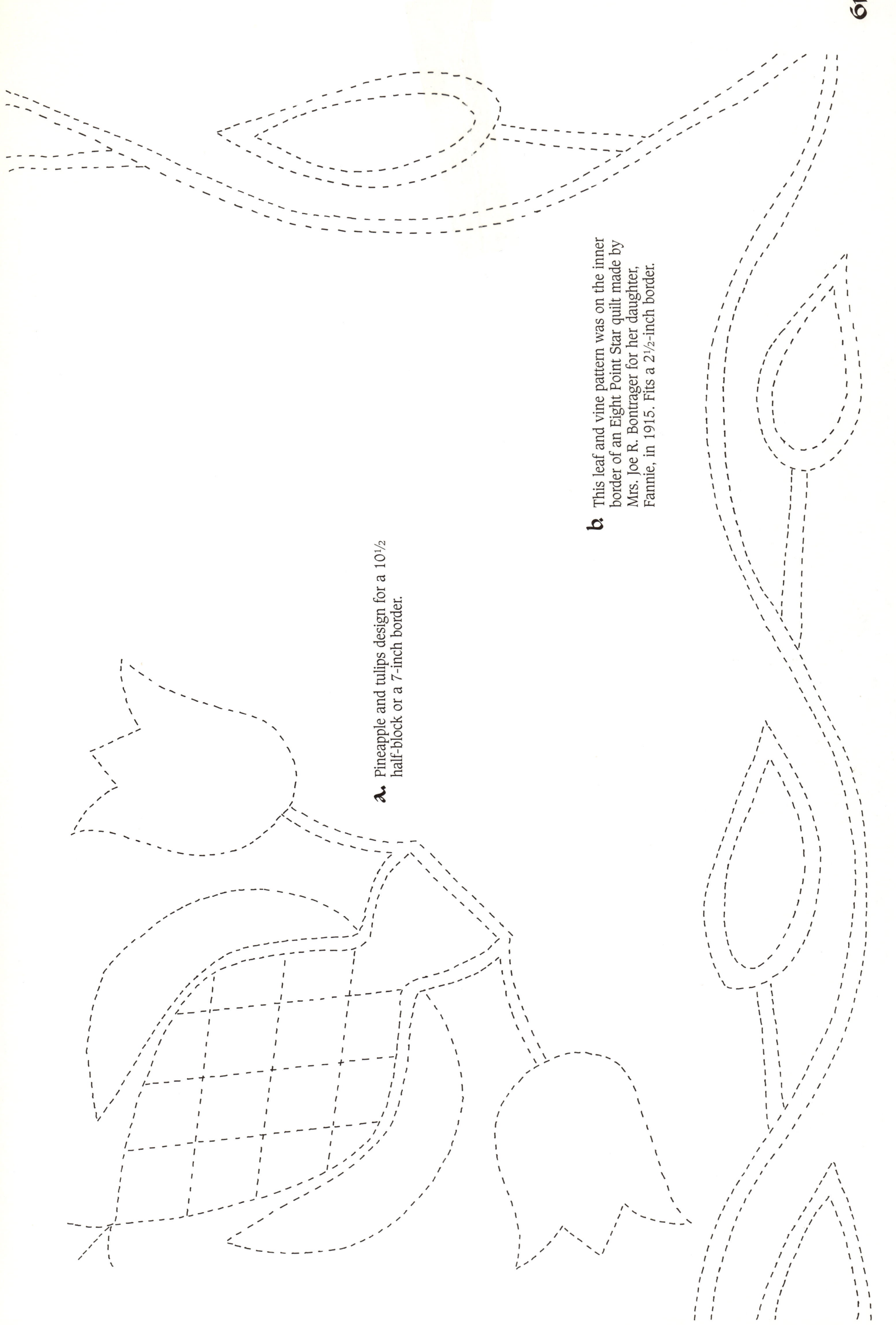

a. Pineapple and tulips design for a 10½ half-block or a 7-inch border.

b. This leaf and vine pattern was on the inner border of an Eight Point Star quilt made by Mrs. Joe R. Bontrager for her daughter, Fannie, in 1915. Fits a 2½-inch border.

a. Little star for a 3½-inch square.

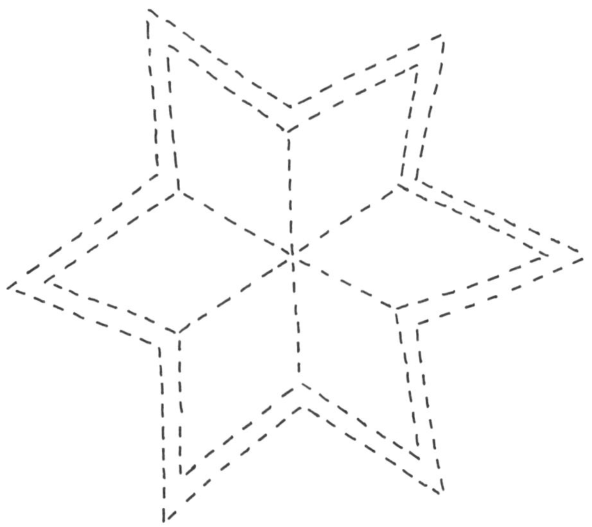

b. A lovely loopy tulip design for a 6-inch border. Dates from approximately 1915.

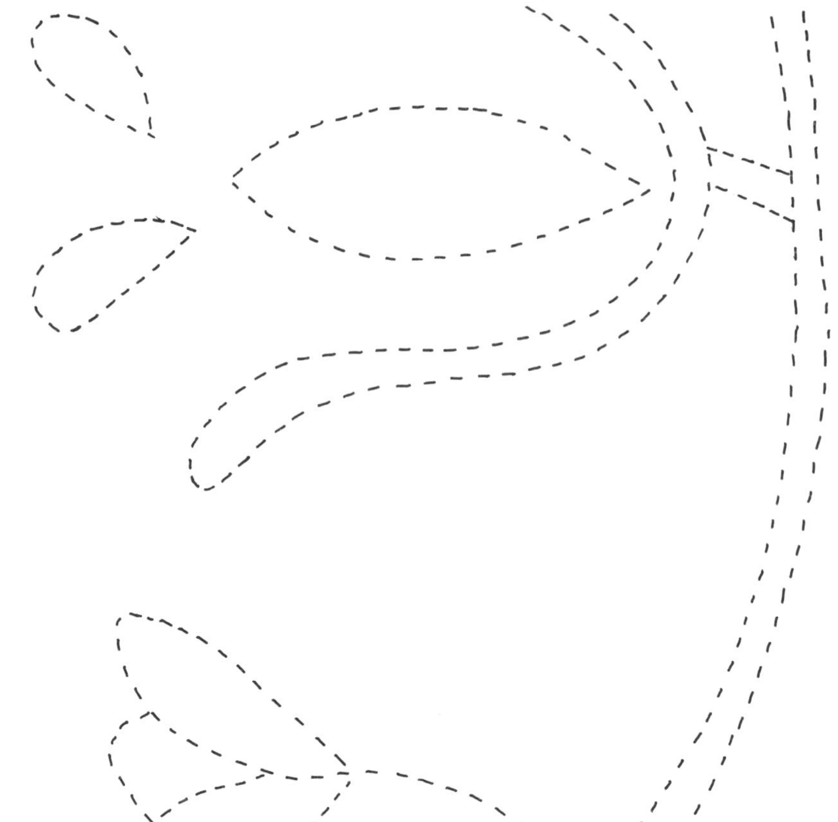

This is a wonderful design to end this book. From a quilt made by Melinda Yoder of Thomas, Oklahoma in 1917. Melinda never married and was famous as a fine quiltmaker in her community. For a 9-inch border. The little drawing illustrates how the stencil was reversed to produce a balanced design.

Finding the Right Size Design

This index is to help you find the designs in this book that will fit your block or border. These designs fit comfortably (¼ to ½-inch margin) in the sizes listed. A quick and easy tool for finding the ideal design is to cut a tracing paper square the size of your block. Leaf through the book and place the block over designs you like. Since the design will show through the tracing paper, you can visualize what that design will look like on your quilt. Refer to Playing with Patterns (pp. 38-39) for even more quilting possibilities.

The designs are listed with the page number first, followed by the letter designating the design, i.e. 32a. Half-blocks (blocks cut on the diagonal) are listed under "Blocks."

For Blocks 10 inches or larger:
7, 9a, 12b, 13, 15, 16a and b, 17, 20, 21b, 24b, 27b, 34, 35, 40, 41, 49, 52, 55, 60, 61a

For Blocks 6 inches to 10 inches:
8a and b, 9b, 12a, 14a, 16b, 19 a and c, 21a, 28a, 29a and b, 31, 32a and b, 33a and b, 34, 42a and b, 48, 50b, 51a, 53, 56b, 58b

For Blocks less than 6 inches:
14b, 44a, 51b, 62a

For Borders 8 inches or wider:
10, 11, 12a, 17, 37, 41, 43, 46, 47, 55, 63

For Borders 4 inches to 7½ inches:
18a, 21b, 22, 23a and b, 25, 26, 28a and b, 45 a and b, 49, 50a, 54, 56 and 57a, 59, 61a, 62b

For Borders less than 4 inches:
19b, 44b, 58a, 61b

About the Author

Following a doctor's recommendation in 1972 to find a hobby to alleviate stress, Pepper Cory stumbled over her first quilt at a garage sale. "As we drove home, I held the old quilt on my lap, stroked it, examined the blocks and wondered over the tiny quilting stitches. I had a sudden thought—I wanted to do this—make quilts—and furthermore, that I **could** do it. I have never experienced such a sure purpose of thought and enthusiasm. I had found my art."

Pepper began teaching quilting in 1975 and opened her shop, Culpepper's Quilts, in 1976. After seven years of teaching and shop-minding, Culpepper's Quilts closed in 1984—with no regrets. In 1985, Pepper published her first book, *Quilting Designs from the Amish*, and this work, *Quilting Designs from Antique Quilts* is her latest endeavor. When not researching quilting patterns and writing, Pepper designs quilts for special customers and teaches workshops all over the country. You can contact her by writing to:

Pepper Cory
c/o The Quilt Studio
210 Abbott, Suite 44
East Lansing, Michigan 48823

Sources & Resources

Carrow and McNerney Country Antiques
P.O. Box 125
Winnetka, Illinois 60093

The Collection of Mary Strickler's Quilt
Linda Ruether/Julie Silber
c/o Julie Silber
Esprit De Corp
900 Minnesota St.
San Francisco, CA 94107

Fisher's Antiques
Morton Street
Shipshewana, Indiana 46565
By chance or appointment.

Bruce and Charlotte Riddle Antiques
116 West Broadway
Bardstown, Kentucky 40004
Chance or appointment.